Quick Clips

Elk Mountain Press
1101 Village Road, LL-1-B
Carbondale, Colorado 81623
(970) 963-9449
First Printing 1997

Library of Congress Catalog Card Number: 97-061442

Illustrated by John McMullen
ISBN 1-887216-08-1

Printed in the United States of America
10 9   8   7   6   5   4   3   2   1

Table of contents

ROCK CLIMBING

SPORT CLIMBING AND BOULDERING

AID AND WALL CLIMBING

KNOTS AND ROPES

RAPPELLING

ICE, MIXED, AND MOUNTAINEERING

Tricksters and fools

Climbers are natural tricksters. We are always looking for better, safer, easier ways to skin the cat. But we could never have guessed that when Quick Clips began in *Climbing* some six years ago the office would swim in tips submitted by our readers. They poured in by the sackful. The burden on the local post office was such that there were several insanities. They begged us to cancel the column, but we are a mean people.

The great flood meant we could cull only the choicest tips, and have now pulled together the best of the best (and a few new ones) and bound them in the book you now hold. For instance, who would have thought you could make an expanding chock from a puffer fish? This one ran as a joke some years back. We got some angry mail about cruelty to animals, but here it is again because we really like it, and think you will, too. Or convert a K-Mart cot into a portaledge? Or throw together an emergency bolt kit from hardware-store parts? Not I.

If I have a regret, it is that we were not able to share some of the gut-splitting laughter given us by the wacky tips that didn't make print. Perhaps I can share a few with you now? Good.

My favorite was the one from the fellow who recommended a diet of raw eggs, twigs, and insects. The benefits, he said, were weight control and increased power. A prisoner from some joint in California supplied us with a new way to rope solo. You take two pieces of gear, runner them to your harness, and leap-frog them up the face. I often wonder if that nugget of enlightenment didn't cost him another five to 10 in lockup. Yet another good citizen suggested you fill your car trunk with bricks so your headlights would cast farther during those all-night drives. As a bonus, he wrote that the flicking headlights of all those oncoming cars would help keep you awake. That guy is probably figuring out his own way over the wall right about now. And then there was the old chalk-in-the-panty-hose chalk ball tip. We probably got that one a couple dozen times. Never ran it — none of us were willing to sacrifice a perfectly good pair of hose in the name of fact checking.

Maybe next time.

Duane Raleigh
Quick Clips Editor

Rock climbing

Spread 'em

Here's a tip for extracting protection that is locked in the jaws of an expanding flake. Take a camming unit and place it behind the flake, just above or below the piece you want to remove. Weight the unit. Voila, the expanding action of the cam spreads the flake, letting you remove the stuck piece of gear. Since the cam can blow out unexpectedly, be sure you tie yourself off if you are on rappel.

— Jonathan Feldshuh
Barrytown, New York

Real rockcraft

How may times have you run out of runners? Or dropped your belay device? Or not had enough nuts or cams? Being caught short is a drag, but some clever improvisation and a few tricks can bail you out of a fix.

Your rope zig-zags up the wall and you desperately need a runner, but you've used them all. Convert your wired or slung nuts into quickdraws by sliding down the nut and clipping both ends. If your gear sling or chalkbag belt is runner-strength, you can also use it as an improvised runner. If you've exhausted all the other options, use the slings on your cams as short draws: clip two carabiners to each sling and let the cam hang.

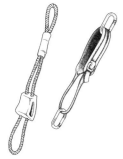

Real rockcraft. Convert wired nuts into emergency runners by sliding down the nut and clipping both ends. Runner-strength gear slings also make improv slings.

Worse case: you drop your descending device at the start of a rappel. You also dropped most of your carabiners, so a carabiner-brake rappel is out of the question. Don't panic; if you still have one large locking carabiner or two standard ovals you can use the Munter hitch. Arrange the hitch with both ropes overlapping each other, not side by side as you would for a double-rope belay. A word of caution: the Munter hitch puts more twists in your rope that Stephen King puts in a plot. To work out the kinks, let your properly equipped partner rap last.

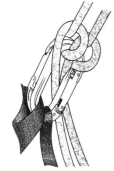

Real rockcraft. The Munter hitch used for double-rope rappel. Don't forget to reverse and oppose the carabiner gates.

Before cams, even before slider nuts, climbers stacked nuts and hexes to broaden their range and protect parallel cracks. You can do the same when you find yourself strung out without the right size or sort of pro. Doing so is simple: fit two nuts together (one upside down), slip them into the crack, tug on the rightside-up nut, and then clip it.

The guidebook said the pitch ate gear, but you still didn't bring enough. Time to get creative. Try wedging your belay plate, a carabiner, nut tool, or sturdy pebble into a crack and tying it off. And

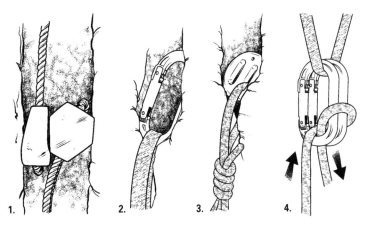

Real rockcraft. (From left to right) 1. Stacked nuts fill the gap when nothing else will do. 2. & 3. A carabiner and belay plate jammed as protection. 4. The one-directional Garta Hart.

don't forget the Eastern bloc standard of jammed knots; if the knots on your slings are too small, double the knot over itself to increase its girth.

Yikes. You thought you could haul your day pack hand-over-hand, but two pitches up you are so cooked you can hardly clip the anchors. Time for the Garta-Hart knot, a handy one-directional slipping knot that — though it doesn't have the mechanical advantage of a pulley — locks itself off, letting you rest between pulls.

— Fred Knapp
Boulder, Colorado

Removable objects

You are on your first big multi-pitch route. The last 10 pitches are sweet memories, and now with only two pitches to go, you can taste that first beer at the Mountain Room Bar. Seconding the crux hand crack, you reach the crucial #2.5 Friend that your partner hastily stuffed below the roof. Unfortunately, the Friend is overcammed, and after 30 minutes of fiddling, the piece is really stuck. With darkness approaching, you have to leave it. There goes your beer money.

So it doesn't happen again, here are a few tips for

Removable objects. Pre-slinging your triggers is an easy way to head off fixed camming units.

removing those troublesome camming units.

Equipment. You don't need much, but you do need a nut tool (it helps to have two) to extract stuck gear. Get one that has both a sturdy hooked end that can snag trigger bars, and a flat end that you can smack with a carabiner, large nut, or cam.

Removable objects. A sturdy nut tool is worth its weight in gold.

Technique. Getting yourself into the correct position is essential to clean gear quickly and efficiently. When you arrive at a piece of pro, find the hand holds and foot holds that the leader used to place the gear. If you can't stand on them or hang from them long enough to extract the gear, climb a bit higher or reverse to better holds that let you reach, and see, the placement.

Get comfortable, scope the placement and imagine how the piece went in. Most camming units get plugged straight in, but occasionally they are slotted into an opening, then moved to a different location. If removing the piece isn't obvious, ask the leader for any special trick he used to key in the placement. With a little beta that hopelessly stuck piece can come right out.

If there's a chance you might drop the gear trying to clean it, clip a long sling to it, and clip the sling to your harness or rack. In strenuous situations it's best to leave the gear clipped to the rope and let it stack up at your tie-in knot until you reach a stance where you can reorganize.

Removable objects. Use a nut tool to hook and pull down an inverted cam.

Problematic stuck gear may take both hands to remove. Unless you're at a no-hands stance, you'll either have to take tension on the rope, clip yourself to a higher placement and hang on that, or leave the placement, finish the pitch, and lower back down and get it.

Problems and Solutions. SLCDs typically get stuck one of three ways.

1) They "walk" or get pushed so deep in the

crack you can't reach the trigger. 2) One or two of the cams over-rotates (inverts) and jams upside-down like a nut. 3) The piece was crammed so tightly (overcammed) in the placement that pulling the trigger doesn't retract the cams.

Prevention is the ticket for cam walking. The leader should use runners to keep the rope from rocking the placement, and take care not to kick the piece deeper into the crack as he climbs past it. Also, the leader should resist the temptation to set the unit, then give the shaft an extra nudge, burying the unit past the trigger. If the leader can't reach the trigger, chances are, neither will the second. As a final protective measure, you can rig your camming units with a thin cord that lets you retract the cams without being able to reach the trigger.

Removable objects. To extract a buried unit, loop wired nuts over the trigger.

When a cam is buried to where you can't reach the cheater cord, try hooking the cord or trigger with your nut tool. Another alternative is to loop wire nuts over both ends of the trigger. These delicate operations are two-handed procedures, so be prepared to take tension.

Inverted cams are usually caused when you thrash around trying to remove the unit. Remain cool and collected, and you may never face cam inversion. But when you do, pull the trigger to retract the other cams, then, with the trigger held tight, take a nut tool and either pull down the inverted cam or push it up even more to reduce its profile. The unit should come out. If it doesn't, try easing it to a wider place in the crack.

Overcammed units are almost always the fault of the leader, who, panic-stricken, crammed in a piece that was too large for the placement. When you arrive at an overcammed piece, curse the leader, then settle down to business. Retract the trigger as much as you can, hold it there, then take a nut tool and pull down the cams to retract them even more. If you can reach the cams with your fingers, so much the better. If this method doesn't work, you still have a couple of options before pronouncing the piece fixed. Pull the trigger tight and try wrenching the piece out. That failing, try shoving the unit to a wider section in the crack.

When the cams are completely retracted and still won't budge, the situation is probably hopeless. As a last resort, sling the trigger, hang from it, and whack the stem with a hammer or a large nut. Sometimes the sudden shock of the blow will cause the unit to slip.

One last bit of advice. If the piece will not move either up or down, hook the top of it with your nut tool and try to slide the unit out sideways.

For the majority of placements, cleaning SLCDs is simple, and when it isn't persistence can pay big dividends. Few things in climbing are as disheartening as leaving behind a unit only to return later and find it gone - removed by someone who knows the tricks.

— *Bruce Hildenbrand*
Mountain View, California

Take the squeeze out of boots

The overwhelming joy of new rockshoes is inevitably forgotten the moment you cram them on your feet for their first spin on the rock. The excruciating pain lasts day after miserable day until finally the shoes have stretched to a perfect fit. Take those babies straight home, lock the doors and turn on the faucet. What you want to do is completely wet the boots in lukewarm water; never use hot water because the soles could delaminate (the likelihood of this occurring is slim, but why take the chance). Squeeze those puppies on your feet, tighten up the laces and sit on your butt. Leave the boots on for as long as you can, occasionally standing and walking around. The idea is to give the boots long enough to stretch and conform to your foot so you can avoid pain, frustration, and more pain. The result will leave a smile on your face, not some ugly grimace.

— *Phillip Benningfield*
Old Snowmass, Colorado

Water haul

Everyone wants the perfect water container, but we seem to overlook the obvious when we polish off one of those "boxes" of wine. Next time, remove the plastic bladder and save it for use as a water bottle. The bladder is lightweight, compresses when it's empty, and when it's full, can assume any shape for fitting in your pack.

— *Mark E. Hotaling*
Fort Collins, Colorado

Sounds fishy

Puffers are lightweight and disposable protection for finger and larger cracks. The puffer, or blowfish, is the small saltwater creature capable of inflating its body until it resembles a globe.

Load a wicker creel with five to 15 fish (remove skin spines), prefitting each with a neoprene or C-4 sleeve. On route, simply pluck out a puffer, hold inside the crack, and scream. Frightened, the puffer will swell, creating a secure but temporary chockstone around which you loop a 1/2-inch tie-off. Our puffers have remained lodged for the duration of full-rope Devils Tower leads — the moving rope and rattling carabiners keep the puffer on edge.

Sounds fishy. The puffer fish returns.

You can clean puffers several ways. First, a hard upward jerk on the sling can dislodge the fish, provided it is weakened or dehydrated. If not, a well-sharpened Super Long Dong pops them, in the messier sense of the word. Better, the little fellas will deflate if you tickle them on the chin with a toothbrush.

Warning: don't chow the puffers. Unless prepared meticulously, these little blowfish are extremely poisonous.

— *Bart Cannon*
Saint Paul, Minnesota

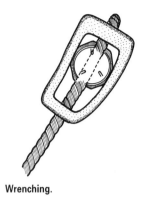

Wrenching.

Wrenching

Have you ever been ready to tighten down a bolt when you discovered you forgot your wrench? Before you panic, check your gear rack — for some bolts, like the Rawl five-piece, the inside of a #12 or #13 Stopper or #5 Hexentric works fine as an improvised wrench.

— Jon Butler
Grand Junction, Colorado

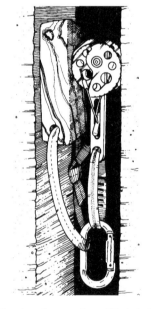

Cam jam. A cam and wood-block stack. Dicey, but better than nothing.

Cam jam

On aid routes with cracks wider than the pieces on your conventional rack, such as El Capitan's *Excalibur*, you can extend the working range of your camming units by bracing them against a block of wood, which serves as a spacer. You can easily "protect" five- and six-inch cracks by stacking a four-inch camming unit with a piece of two-by-four. The wood is cut slightly wider than the cam, roughed up on both sides so it grips, and has a small hole drilled through it for tying a keeper sling. Thicker or thinner blocks will extend your camming range even further. Use this method for aid only, as it isn't strong enough to hold falls, and be sure you hang from the cam, not the wood block.

— Bill Cipher
Aspen, Colorado

Pinned

Number three and four Camalots are great, but they can be a nuisance to carry — it seems like they are always catching on your pants, in brush, and tangling with the rest of the rack. The easy way to solve this is to retract the cams, and slide a pin through the holes at the tips of the outside cams. To remove the pin, simply turn the Camalot so the pin can fall out and squeeze the trigger. A light piece of cord will keep the pin from getting lost.

— *Larry Sallee*
Kingman, Arizona

Pinned. Pin your large Camalots to reduce their bulk.

Sport climbing and bouldering

Threading thoughtfully

Here is a fast, safe method for threading the climbing rope through belay anchors to lower off a route. Clip into your harness with a quickdraw, then clip this to the anchor and hang. While still tied into the rope, pull up a few feet of slack and thread a loop of rope through the ring bolts, and tie an overhand figure-8 knot in it. Now clip this knot into your harness tie-in point or belay loop with a locking carabiner or two carabiners with gates opposed and reversed. Finally, untie your climbing knot, pull the tail out through the lower-off point, unclip the quickdraw, and lower to the deck on the new overhand figure-8.

This method has several advantages over the more common technique of untying and threading the rope end directly through the anchor. It's faster, and there is no danger of dropping the rope. Most importantly, you never have to be off belay or untie. Disadvantages: the lower-off point must accept a double thickness of rope; you are attached to the rope with carabiners for the lower, so be sure to clip into a safe point on your harness and double-check it; and you must lower with several feet of unused rope end dangling from the double figure-8 knot — no big deal unless the pitch is exactly half a ropelength.

— *Mack Johnson*
Bremerton, Washington

Safety in numbers. Simple mistakes lead to disasters.

Safety in numbers

Sloppy belaying, tying in wrong, and improperly rigging a lowering station are the banes of sport and indoor climbing. If you've climbed for any length of time I'll bet you know of, or were involved in, an accident involving simple, avoidable mistakes.

It's time to clean up our act.

Before I took up climbing I was an avid scuba diver. Two more diverse activities I can't imagine, but there is one diving practice that should become commonplace in climbing

— the buddy system. Divers generally dive in pairs, and before they enter the water they check each other's equipment, and give a thumbs-up to acknowledge it's safe to go. Do the same before starting a route. Check yourself, then check your partner. Is his knot tied correctly? Harness buckle doubled back? Belay device properly loaded? Screwgate locked?

When you are belaying, pay attention. Watch the leader. Idle banter and other distractions such as rummaging through your pack for a banana are recipes for broken bones — yours as well as the leader's. More frequently, leaders are dropped because the belayer positioned himself too far out from the crag, preferring that comfy spot in the sun over the proper stance just under the first piece of pro. Choose your belay stance so the loaded rope won't ram you into an overhang or parked car. Also, don't belay on your ass. Stand up, keep your shoes on so you can maneuver over sharp ground, and wear gloves to protect your hands.

When you are climbing, communicate with your belayer — don't assume he knows you need slack or are about to fall. Be especially vocal when you rig a lowering station. And finally, right before you "take" and lower, check that your knot is correctly tied, then establish eye contact with your belayer to make sure he knows what's going on.

— Emma Williams
Manchester, England

Hitting the sauce

The soles of my rock shoes get very dirty. Scrubbing them with a wire brush works OK, but one day I decided there had to be a better way. That's when I found Turtle Wax Bug and Tar Remover, a cleaning compound made for removing tar and the like from cars. I tried it, and it works nicely to make climbing-shoe rubber as sticky clean as new. It is now the secret sauce I use before a scary lead or hard bouldering session.

— Nick Telischak
Belvedere, California

It lives beneath the stairs

A convenient place to build a climbing cave in your home is under the stairs. This is an excellent place for those with limited space. Use wood screws to attach 3/4-inch plywood (be sure T-nuts are in place) to the stair supports. You may need some two-by-fours to brace the mid-section of the plywood if it flexes. Although small, this wall provides good power training.

— *Brian Mecham*
Ogden, Utah

One-arm helper

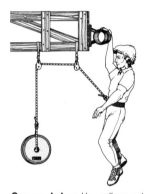

One-arm pullups are a goal for many climbers. Problem is, most of us are too weak to even attempt one. Solution: suspend a weight from one end of a rope that runs overhead through two pulleys. Clip your harness to the other end of the rope. Now when you try a one-arm pull-up the weight will help lift you. As you get stronger you can decrease the weight until one day you no longer need any weight at all.

One-arm helper. Use pulleys and a counterweight to develop your one-arm power.

— *Blake Madden*
Augusta, Georgia

Go figure

Here's a simple way to change out belayers while someone is climbing, requiring one belay device. If you are using a Tuber, Sticht plate, Figure-8, or similar device, (not a GRIGRI), merely have the soon-to-be belayer clip her locking carabiner into the same bight of rope the belayer's locking carabiner is clipped to. The new belayer can thus immediately put the climber on while the original belayer unclips.

Go figure. The safe way to switch belayers using only one belay device.

— *Lisa Raleigh*
Milton Falls, Colorado

Stick 'em up

When you are working a sport climb that requires stick clipping the first bolt, keeping that bolt clipped when you pull the rope for a redpoint attempt can be a problem. Stay clipped by tramming into the rope above that bolt, and then lower to the ground. Now when you pull the rope, it is still clipped through the first bolt.

— *Jeff Jackson*
Austin, Texas

Stick 'em up.

Overhanging problem

Cleaning quickdraws off overhanging bolted routes is problematic. As you lower from the top anchors, you swing away from the rock and the quickdraws. Solve this problem by clipping a quickdraw to your harness and "tramming" into the rope leading to your belayer. As you lower, you'll still swing away from the rock, but the rope running through the quickdraws will go with you. When you're level with the quickdraw have your belayer lock you off and then use the rope to pull yourself in.

When tension from the rope makes unclipping the quickdraw difficult, unload the rope by hanging from a hold on

Overhang problem. "Tram" into the rope to clean quickdraws off an overhanging route.

the climb. Remain trammed into the rope until the last quickdraw is cleaned. You can prevent a large swing by remaining trammed in until you reach the ground; this will pull your belayer out from the rock, so make sure he is well anchored.

— *Jeff Jackson*
Austin, Texas

Super soaker.

Super soaker

It's common courtesy to scrub chalk-caked or dirty holds after you have finished a session on the boulders. But sometimes the holds are out of reach, inaccessible, or such a mess that a mere brush just doesn't cut it. That's when you break out the pressure sprayer and hose those crimpers down. A pump-up pressure sprayer, like the type made for nuking bugs and weeds, will sanitize holds 20 feet away, works like a Water Pik to flush out pockets and other hard-to-reach holds, and also removes all the chalk — an attribute worth noting in areas where "civilians" take offense to chalk smears.

You can get a cheapo sprayer, which does a fair job, at Wal-Mart for under $10, but the higher-pressure models do better and last longer. The sprayer is best suited to bouldering, but it also works for zapping sport routes.

— Terrence Middleby
Point Pleasant, Pennsylvania

Getting the brush

Your psyching for one more burn on the local bouldering testpiece. It would be nice to brush off those slopers, but you'd need a step ladder to reach them. For under $15 and a trip to the hardware store you can devise a tool to scour those grips with ease.

Make a "bubba" brush from a 1/2-inch electrical conduit pipe, which is rigid enough for vigorous scrubbing. Conduit comes in 10-foot lengths, and you can cut it down to the desired length (six feet is adequate for most boulders) with a hacksaw. Once you have your stick length, cap both ends with a 90-degree PVC joint (1/2-inch outside diameter) so

Getting the brush. The ultimate bubba brush.

that the ends point in opposite directions. Attach a curved grout brush, available in most large grocery stores, to one end of the conduit with two small hose clamps. You can, of course, substitute a toothbrush for the grout brush, but the stiffer bristles of the latter do a better job and last longer.

After brushing the out-of-reach holds you can blow off the residual chalk or dust by puffing down the pipe using the bottom PVC joint as a mouthpiece. Also, for clipping high first bolts, you can convert the pole into a "cheater stick" by clamping a spring-loaded clamp to the blowing end.

— *Chris Goplerud*
Basalt, Colorado

Brace yourself

Even if you don't do pockets now, chances are you'll visit one of the new climbing areas where mono pulls are the game. So, you need to learn to tape your fingers, just in case. Start with a 12-inch strip of tape, torn about 1/2-inch wide. Place the end of the strip on the back of your finger above the middle knuckle. Make one complete wrap making sure you cover the front edge of the crease under your knuckle as you complete the circle. On the second pass, diagonal across the crease of your finger. Now, bend your finger at a 45-degree angle and bring the tape up behind the

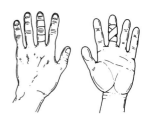
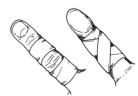

Brace yourself. Fortify your tendons with tape.

knuckle. Do not cover the knuckle. Straighten the finger and complete one full wrap behind the knuckle, making sure to cover the back edge of the crease during the wrap. On the second pass, diagonal back across the crease, bend the finger again at a 45-degree angle, and come up on the front side of the knuckle, ending where you began. Armed with this tape job your finger is free to move, yet is protected and splinted for whenever you have to use your "mono gun."

— *Jack Mileski*
The Great Beyond

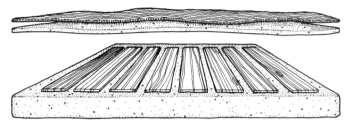

Smashing. Quarter-inch plywood sandwiched in a homemade spotting pad distributes the impact of long drops.

Simply smashing

Judy knows I try, but I just can't flash V6. Predictably, I spend as much time in the air as on the rock. After one particularly savage fall I decided I needed a spotting pad. But my old brittle bones needed more cush than a mere scrap of carpet and a hunk of foam could provide. The solution came to me while I watched girl's gymnastics on the tube. If those bony waifs can rip off a triple backflip and then slam unharmed into the floor, I told myself, then that must be some killer special floor. It is. Gym floors are matt-covered plywood with springs underneath. Using that theme, I was able to create a dynamite smash pad. Here's how I did it.

I got a 4-inch-thick open-cell foam pad to serve as the "springs." My pad is twin-bed size (about $30 at the Surplus), but any dimension will do. Next, I rounded up a full-length Ensolite-type pad ($8 at the Surplus), scrounged a half sheet of 1/4-inch plywood, a gallon of carpet glue ($25 at the hardware), and enough closed-loop Berber carpet to cover both sides of the pad ($15 at a carpet store; don't get shag, it collects sticks and leaves). The initial outlay of about $80 was cheaper than even one spinal fusion, and the pad doubles as a cozy bed.

I cut the plywood into 3-inch-wide by 2 1/2-foot-long slats and glued them on top of the foam, making sure to leave at least two inches of open space between each rib. I kept the ribs several inches back from the edges of the pad, so I wouldn't clip my ankles on the wood. The slats are the key to the design. They flex, absorbing some impact, and also spread the shock across the mat. And best of all, the ribs smooth out jagged landings by keeping sticks and boulders from stabbing through. Next, I glued the Ensolite over the ribs and then cut and glued the carpet over that. Finishing it out, I glued carpet on the underbelly of the foam.

This pad is stouter than most, and Verm found it a tad jarring for short drops. That's easy to fix, simply flip the thing over so the ribs are against the ground and the "soft" side faces up. The Smasher, however, is best for long bombs.

This whole rig weighs a meaty 15 pounds. I fold mine in half and lug it around, although the pump probably costs me a boulder problem or two. A better design would have shoulder straps, but I'll leave that up to you.

— Duane Raleigh
Milton Falls, Colorado

Soft touch

Do you dread waiting for your new shoes to "soften up"? Are your new slippers a little too stiff? If so, you can speed up the softening process by simply placing your shoes, sole up, on a hard flat surface, and whacking the sole with a hammer for a few minutes. This will break down the midsole, making the shoe more flexible.

— Jim Thornburg
Berkeley, California

Aid and wall climbing

Let the games begin

Once again you are stuck on a portaledge in a storm with nothing to do. Not anymore. How about a rousing round of time-killing backgammon?

Prepare ahead at home by taking a permanent magic marker and drawing a backgammon board onto your portaledge or sleeping pad. Indicate where to place the pieces in case you forget, and go buy a pair of dice. Now, next time you get stuck on a wall all you need to do is round up 15 black and 15 white pebbles, place them on the "board" and toss the dice.

— *Boris Mannsfeld*
Denver, Colorado

Wham bam

How many times have you been in a situation — a manky rappel anchor needs a backup, or a key bolt is missing from a ladder — where you needed an emergency bolt kit, but left it behind because it weighed too much? Or you never owned one because you didn't feel like burning $75 on a drill that you'd seldom, if ever, use.

Well, stick out your neck no more. Here's a simple, inexpensive way to whip together a lightweight, compact emergency bolt kit for under $10.

Go to the hardware store and purchase:
    13mm combination wrench
    8mm by 4cm hex-head bolt (any grade will do)
    Three 8mm nuts
    Four washers to fit the bolt
Go to a climbing shop and purchase:
    One Petzl self-drilling "Spitz" bolt
    One Petzl cap screw and washer for bolt
    One bolt hanger to fit Petzl bolt (Petzl aluminum hangers are lightest)

Wham bam. An inexpensive emergency bolt kit.

The wrench, hex bolt, nuts, and washers will make up the drill holder. To assemble, slide two washers onto the bolt, then tightly screw down a nut. Fit the closed end of the combo wrench around the nut, and add the other two washers. Screw on the last two nuts. Done.

Screw the Spitz bolt onto the end of the holder and you are ready to drill. Hammer on the holder while you rotate it clockwise. Periodically remove the drill and blow out the hole to prevent the bit from binding. Total drill time should be around 10 minutes in granite.

Once the hole is drilled, unscrew the

Wham bam. The Petzl Spitz bolt.

Spitz bolt from the holder. If the Spitz has seized on the hanger, put it back in the hole and hammer on it while you rotate it counterclockwise. The Spitz should work loose.

Last, set the expansion cone (supplied with bolt) into the bolt's expanding end, tap the bolt into the hole, and screw on the hanger and cap screw. Enjoy, but remember — a single bolt is not a fail-safe anchor.

— Sean Issac
Canmore, Canada

New old trick

Everyone knows the old trick of cinching a wired nut over a hangerless bolt. Problem is, an outward pull can pop the cable off the bolt, sending you on the big ride. There is a better way — use a knifeblade. While you aren't likely to have a blade on your free rack, you will have at least one with you on a big wall, which is where most of us find ourselves shy of hangers anyway.

To use this technique, unscrew the nut on the bolt and slip the blade's lightening/tie-off hole over the shaft. (If the bolt is the solid-head type you're out of luck; try the wired nut or a tie-off.) Now screw the nut back on. Presto. Clip the blade's offset eye just as you would a regular hanger; with 1/4- and 3/8-inch bolts you'll need a washer to keep the blade pinned tight — if the scum before you chucked the washer and you're fresh out, try using a RURP as a washer.

— Pete Takeda
Boulder, Colorado

New old trick. A knifeblade bolt hanger.

Higher ground

Two-thousand feet up El Cap, you are standing in aiders, stretching for a slammer horizontal crack. Alas, you come up a foot short. Now you must grit your teeth and fuss with a tiny rotten seam.

But maybe not. Before you reach for the copperheads, take a look at your feet. Chances are, you are low in the steps, and simply moving a step up will get you to that crack, and merrily on your way.

Creating and maintaining opposition between your feet and harness is the key to highstepping. Here's how: with your feet in the second or third steps, clip a daisy chain or sling from your harness to the gear you are weighting. Now, put a foot in the next higher step, and, using one hand to help pull and balance on the daisy and the other to grab any usable face holds, step up. Alternately, you can put your feet level in the same high steps, and "frog" into position.

Higher ground. Lever up, then reach.

Once you are in the high step, the daisy or sling must be stretched taut so your feet and harness are in tight opposition. Any slack, even as little as a single carabiner's length in the sling, will let you sag back down. Practice with daisy/sling length until you have the system fine tuned.

The above tactic works fine on vertical to just past vertical rock, but steeper than that and you'll also need to rig a daisy chain so you can opposition off your chest harness or gear sling. Again, adjust the daisy length so it is tight when you highstep and are fully extended.

Lastly, highstepping creates a savage outward pull on the placement, so watch out, especially when you are nutting or hooking.

— Chris Breemer
Aromas, California

Bombs away

Once a treat, the days of crapping off Yosemite big-walls and into space are over. Recent regulations require that solid human waste be carried up the wall and disposed of in proper receptacles on the valley floor. And in Zion, the area's fragile ecosystem makes defecating in the wild irresponsible. Here's the beta on making durable, hanging poop tubes using materials available from any hardware store.

Parts list:
4-inch-by-10-foot (standard length) white PVC nonperforated sewer pipe ($6)
4-inch PVC cap ($1)
4-inch PVC threaded adapter and screw cap ($4)
4-ounce can of PVC cement ($2)
Large hose clamp ($1.50)
Old sling

To assemble, cut a 2.5-foot length of the 4-inch pipe and glue the cap and threaded adapter onto each end. (Alternately you can use a screw cap on each end, enabling you to hose out the tube after each wall.) Use the hose clamp to attach the sling so you can hang the unit upright. Stick the test plug on top, and you're ready to go. But don't go directly into the tube. Equip a number of large paper bags with toilet paper. After you use each bag, toss it in the tube for safekeeping, and once you're back on the ground, dispose of the contents at an RV dump. Lime or a deodorizer found at RV supply shops will keep the stink down.

— *John Middendorf*
San Francisco, California

Bombs away. The do-it-yourself poop tube.

Shelter from the storm

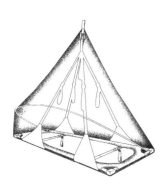

Shelter from the storm. Fly straps and a tent pole make storm-bound bivies secure and roomy.

Shelter from the storm. Tie in with slack so rainwater drains away from your bag.

This past winter a friend and I attempted El Cap's *Lost in America*. We hoped for Yosemite's typical mild conditions, but it rained on us continuously. The fly on our portaledge leaked and flooded us with ice water. We bailed from five pitches up.

It wasn't until my fourth attempt (it rains every time I get on a wall in the Valley) that I climbed the route. Even then it rained for seven of the eight climbing days. Out of all this drenching craziness, I learned a few tricks to make life a bit more pleasant when the weather turns sour.

First, use a synthetic sleeping bag. This might sound like common sense, but until I spent a miserable night in a lumpy, wet down bag, I had always figured that a Gore-Tex down bag was adequate. It isn't.

Next, seal all the seams on your portaledge fly with Seam Grip — the only stuff that really works. Coat the stitching inside and out.

While you are dinking with the rainfly, sew two quick-release Fastex buckles with straps, crossways about a foot from each end. The straps let you anchor the fly underneath the portaledge so it can't blow up in updrafts.

The real key to being comfortable in a storm, however, is to take an 11-foot, shock-corded aluminum tent pole (use a longer pole if you have a two-man ledge) and set it up inside the ledge as shown. The pole makes the ledge extra roomy and keeps the soaked fly fabric from sagging or slapping you in the face. Set the pole on the outside of the suspension straps, and, to prevent the pole from jumping out of place, duct tape a large alligator clip to each end and clip these to the bed fabric, cables, or cord.

One last bit of advice, tie in with a generous loop of slack that can dangle below the bed, and clip a piece of gear or two to the loop to hold it down. The loop will funnel water away from you rather that channel it into your sleeping bag, as happens if you tie in short.

There you have it. Next time you get caught in a storm and your portaledge starts bucking, you can relax and imagine that you're some crusty old cowboy.

— Cameron Lawson
Geyersville, California

Jug safety

You work during the week, but have a project going on the weekends. You leave fixed ropes hanging for weeks at a time, and when you come back to jumar them, you're always worried that the wind or a rat might have chewed them to shreds. Instead of biting your lip and jugging anyway, have your partner belay you on another rope while you jug the tatty rope. Slap in gear every 20 or so feet, depending on the state of your fixed line.

— Cameron Burns
Basalt, Colorado

Heads up

Here's a technique for making self-equalizing aluminum or copperheads for extremely thin placements where a single head won't hold body weight. Construct them as follows: assuming you have a Nikkopress and the cables and swages, take a standard-length copperhead cable and swage a head on each end. Slip another swage over the cable so that the cable forms a "U". Don't crimp this swage, but leave it loose so it can "float," after you paste in both heads.

— Randy Leavitt
San Diego, California

Heads up.
Equalizing
copperheads.

Going sideways in style. Clip clean traverses for efficient — and safe — going.

Going sideways in style

Cleaning a traverse on a wall can be an extremely demanding task. Try to jumar sideways, and you are begging for the upcoming pieces to rip out. And when a piece does rip along the traverse you then have to either replace it, or lower out on the piece just before it. Both options are time consuming — and avoidable.

Typically, the best way to clean a traverse is to clip across the pieces using your aiders as if you were leading. Keep your jumars on the rope and slide them ahead of you — don't weight them — as a running belay. As a added precaution, back-tie frequently. With any luck your leader has tested each piece, enabling you to clip across quickly without incident. An option is to have the leader put you on belay and reel in the slack as you clip across. For this method to work, though, the leader must have his hands free, which means he will have to delay hauling.

In either case, be extremely careful when you clean an expanding traverse. Start whaling on a pin while you are hanging on a rickety head, and you may well get some flight time on the other sharp end of the rope.

— Mark Synnott
Jackson, New Hampshire

Best of a bad thing

If the aid placement you need already has a broken copper-head or RURP clogging it, try tapping a beak on top of the RURP or into the copperhead itself. This trick is much faster that chiseling out the old piece, and can be easier on the rock.

— *Clay Hilferty*
San Carlos, California

Best of a bad thing.

Hooker heaven

Driving pins is notoriously hard on rock, but you really want to get up the Titan's *Sundevil Chimney*. And that requires slinging iron. Or does it? Next time you come across a pin scar, try lightly tapping a Fish Hook into it. The large hook seats nicely in your standard blown-out hole and doesn't further harm the rock.

— *Jeff Fassett*
Aspen, Colorado

Hooker heaven.
Large hooks make light work of pin scars.

A notch up

Rare is the day when you can send an angle pin to the eye. That's why Warren (or maybe it was Royal) invented the tie-off. Tie-offs work great for reducing leverage on partly driven pins, but they are sneaky devils — the minute you turn your back they slide off, turning A2 into a temple-rupturing fearfest. Needlessly so if you have a bench grinder.

Here's how you do it. Carefully grind a series of shallow (1/8-inch deep) notches on the open channels of each angle pin. Grind slow so you don't overheat the metal, and make sure the resulting notches are baby-skin smooth so they won't cut the tie-off.

Now when you tie-off those pins the webbing can rest in the proper notch, and stay put.

— *Onan J. Goat*
Hell's Kitchen, New York

A notch up.

Keeping your head

You find lots of fixed gear on big-wall trade routes, much of which is unusable. When confronted with a copperhead with a broken cable you have to laboriously dig it out and replace it, or look for another option. A simple solution is to take a #2 rivet hanger, slip it over the copperhead's swage, and cinch it up. The placement won't hold a fall, but it will get you to that bomber A1 placement just out of reach.

— *Rex Pieper*
Lake View Terrace, California

Keeping your head. Dead head tie-off.

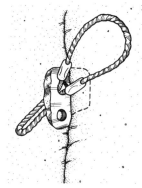

RURP riot

Here's an alternative to clipping the rotten slings on fixed RURPs. Take a number one circlehead, pinch the two swages together, and pound the loop flat so it forms a point. Slide the point through either eye on the RURP and clip to this.

— *Chris Feher*
San Diego, California

RURP riot. A circlehead or wired nut makes a quick replacement for rotten, fixed RURP slings.

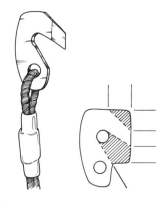

Burp

There I was, on a hard aid lead, and the RURP crack disappeared. I saw a microseam but even a Birdbeak was too large. What did I use? I put in a BURP (beaked ultimate reality piton), which is a RURP cut down with a hacksaw to make a useful mini-Birdbeak.

— *Scott Robertson*
Bozeman, Montana

Burp.

Smart aiders

You'll be up on a big wall for days, hauling loads until your lats look like Arnold's, pounding so many pins your right arm will be twice as big as your left, and trying to land your foot in the flimsy loops of your aiders more times than your partner will insist on replaying that Dead tape.

There's no way around the first situation, but you can remedy the second by coating the steps of your aiders with "Plasti-Dip," available at most hardware stores. Now, your feet will snag the rigid opening of the aider step first try, and the coating will also protect the webbing from abrasion.

— Rex Pieper
Lake View Terrace, California

Wing it

The bolt ladders on popular aid routes are usually missing the hangers and nuts, making two wrenches (one for the leader and another for the second), hangers, and a handful of nuts part of the standard trade-route rack. Simplify things by substituting wing nuts for the regular ones. Wing nuts, besides being easier to start on semi-stripped bolt studs, let you dispense with the wrenches.

— Onan J. Goat
Hell's Kitchen, New York

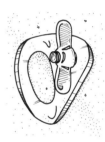

Wing it.

Seeing stars

Wall climbing is the mother of invention. Ask Randy Leavitt. He found that conventional RURPS were far too large for the thin aid lines he eyeballed. He fixed that by grinding RURP blades down to a point. These "stars" seat nicely in placements too narrow for standard RURPS.

— Bill Eagerton
Weatherford, Oklahoma

Seeing stars. Grind a RURP into a point for those desperately thin cracks.

Little big wall

Tired of carrying a full-page topo that turns into a soiled, illegible rag halfway up a long free or aid climb? Fix that by taking the topo to a copy shop and shrinking it to wallet size on a reducing xerox machine. Weatherproof the topo by laminating it with regular 2-inch wide clear packing tape, and punch a hole through it to take a carrying cord. This topo "card" fits neatly in a pocket, or just clip it on the rack.

— Pete Takeda
Boulder, Colorado

Keyed up

Wall climbers are cheapskates — which helps explain why many of the bolts you encounter on big wall routes don't have hangers. Further, judging from most bolts' thrashed condition, it seems that a few sorry individuals have tried to steal the bolts as well. When you encounter a button-head bolt sans hanger, or a hex-head bolt where trashed threads won't let you unscrew the nut and slip on a standard hanger, you need a "keyhole" hanger.

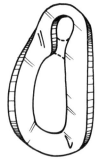

Keyhole hangers are easy to make. First, round up a handful of SMC bolt hangers (they have the best shape for converting). Get some hangers made for 1/4-inch bolts, as well as a few to fit 3/8-inch bolts. Next, clamp the hanger in a vice and use a hacksaw (take the blade off, insert it through the carabiner hole, and then reattach the blade to the handle) to cut out a 1/4- or 3/8-inch slot running from the carabiner hole to the bolt hole.

To use a keyhole hanger, simply slide it over the bolt stud (keyholes also work on some rivets) until it "keys" into place.

Keyed up. A cut-down SMC hanger makes an ideal "keyhole."

— Jimmy Beam
Seattle, Washington

Clean and jerk

Cleaning aid gear — RURPs, copperheads, or pins whaled in behind expando flakes — is usually harder than setting it. I know because I've climbed untold walls with one of your frequent contributors, Onan J. Goat, and he loves to bury gear and then raises Cain when I have trouble getting it out.

Clean and jerk. A funkness device makes removing stubborn or hard-to-reach placements a snap.

I got the last laugh. I made a "funkness" device, which is simply a 2-foot length of #2 copperhead cable with a loop swaged on each end. Now when that old Goat sinks a piece, no problem. If it doesn't succumb to my hammer, I clip one loop of the Device to my hammer head, clip the other loop to the problem piece, give it a burly swipe, and either the piece comes out or it breaks. If your hammer doesn't have a hole in its head, girth hitch a tie-off around the handle and clip to it.

The Funkness also works to test gear. To do this, clip it to the suspect placement and give a downward jerk. Careful — even a light tug generates a surprising amount of impact force; jerk too hard and you can break the cables or slings of good placements, or sprain your wrist. This method works well with really delicate pieces, and has the advantage over traditional bounce testing in that it doesn't shock load the placement you're on if the one you're testing blows.

— *Judy L. Goat*
Hell's Kitchen, New York

Ascender bender

Clip a carabiner through the bottom hole of the ascender, then onto the rope when climbing a horizontal or traversing rope. The carabiner helps prevent the ascender from being twisted off the rope. Also, be certain to tie in with a backup knot at regular intervals along the rope.

— *Duane Raleigh*
Milton Falls, Colorado

Ascender bender.

By hook and by crook

Almost every crag in the West has at least one Harvey T. Carter soft-iron angle piton rusting away in a crack somewhere. While leaving the pin in situ as a relic of days gone by may be the correct thing to do, the wily wall climber will sneak out during a thunderstorm and swipe it. Why? Because soft-iron pins make great ring-angle claws, the large hooks that are mandatory gear on nearly every El Cap nail up.

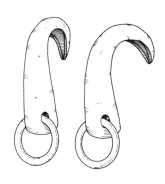

By hook. Soft-iron pitons hammered over into large hooks.

Once you've nabbed the pin, cold forge it into a large hook by pounding it over the edge of a curb or boulder. If you are completely without morals, snag two ring angles. That way you can bend one on a large arc for hooking wide flakes and jugs, and work the other into a sharper bend, which is more secure on smaller, though still large, hooking features.

— *Aleister Kurtz*
London, England

Get the point

It's no secret: most granite wall routes have drilled bathook moves. In most cases, the old pointed Leeper hooks work fine for these placements. However, "modified" edges and bumps are often too thick for the small hooking arm of the Leepers — that's when you pull out your Black Diamond Cliffhanger, which you cleverly redesigned for the occasion by grinding the broad tip into a sharply tapering point. A word of caution: drill a shallow 1/4-inch hole in a boulder and make sure your new bathook fits in it before venturing onto the big stone.

— *Jay Norman*
Dallas, Texas

Cracked up

Remember those Crack'n Ups Chouinard Equipment used to make? You didn't throw your set away, did you? If you did, buy your friend's for cheap before he reads this. With a little alteration Crack'n Ups are indispensable tools on new-wave aid climbs.

To modify a Crack'n Up for aid climbing, merely grind or saw off one of the anchor "blades" so you can drive the piece with a hammer. Now you have the killer weapons, which seat into microcracks (the #0 works in the paper-thin placements) or small pods, where conventional RURPS and knifeblades are dicey or don't fit. These "beaks" may seem spooky at first, but they hold body weight amazingly well and may even slow you down if you take the Big One.

— *Bjorn Dali*
Fresno, California

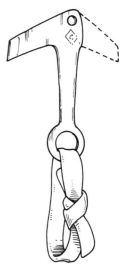

Cracked up. A "beak" made from an old Chouinard Crack'n Up.

Bucket brigade

It seems that no matter how large a haulbag is, it still isn't big enough for everything you want to drag up a big wall. Plastic five-gallon buckets can be used as miniature haulbags by rigging them with webbing so they can hang beneath the haulbags. Buckets are excellent for hauling fragile items such as bananas, and are also great for hauling canned items, which are notorious for wearing through haulbags. As the bucket is emptied it makes a handy garbage container. Before hauling your bucket, make sure the lid is securely fastened and ties on so you don't drop it.

— *Chris Breemer*
Aromas, California

Bucket brigade. Stash your perishables in a plastic bucket rigged for hauling.

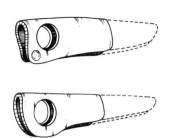

Stumped. For blown-out pin scars, "stumps" may be the solution.

Stumped

While nailing pitches typically get easier due to traffic, once the placements get completely blown out, using them can be more tenuous than ever. For example, the shallow, square peg holes you'll find on many of the popular aid walls in Yosemite and Canyonlands are nearly worthless for conventional hardware. Not so if you have "stumps" — standard 1/2- to 1 1/2-inch angle pitons with the last couple inches of blade sawed off. Stumps seat nicely in shallow pin scars with just a whack or two, don't require a tie-off, and can be very secure.

— Onan J. Goat
Hell's Kitchen, New York

Jug haul

A dropped or forgotten ascender can shut you down. If you find yourself in a jam with only one jumar, don't rappel off — your figure 8 or belay plate double-duties as an ascender.

Put your lone jumar (or whatever ascender you have on the rope) and attach to it with your daisy chain and aiders as usual. Now, put the figure 8 or belay plate on the rope below your jumar and clip to the rope as you would if you were rappelling or belaying. Cinch the rope up snug, and weight the figure 8. Hold yourself with the figure 8, then slide your jumar up and step up in the aider. Your figure 8 is unweighted now, so move it up again by pulling the slack out of the rope. Alternating between the figure 8 and jumar will get you up a rope fairly quickly once you master the technique, although it will be more strenuous than regular jumaring.

Of course you could play it safe, and always carry a set of prusiks as a backup.

— Onan J. Goat
Hell's Kitchen, New York

Jug haul. An improvised ascending system using one mechanical ascender and a figure 8.

Cheap thrills

Big-wall aspirants often possess the drive and cajones to make it up the Big Stone, yet lack the ducats to finance the trip. Several low-tech options can prevent needless investment in costly items like portaledges and haulbags.

Stores like K-Mart and Wal-Mart sell camp cots or chaise lounges for $25 to $40. One of the "ledges," rigged with seven-millimeter perlon suspension makes a surprisingly durable portaledge (one of my K-Mart specials made it up 10 El Cap routes). For added durability, wrap duct tape around the sling knots.

Another money-saving trick: make a functional haulbag by rigging a Navy duffel bag with webbing and then reinforce it with duct tape.

— *Pete Takeda*
Boulder, Colorado

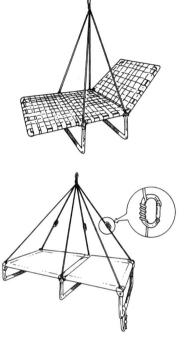

Cheap thrills. The poor-man's portaledge. Use a carabiner wrapped in the suspension to level the bed.

Put the hammer down

Don't have $75 for a wall hammer? An oversized ballpeen hammer from your local hardware store works fine, and only costs around $20. If you have access to a grinder, you can modify the ball side for nailing by grinding it to a pick. Ballpeen hammer handles tend to be long, but it's easy enough to cut the shaft down to your size, and then drill a hole through it for a sling.

— *David Mavancik*
San Jose, California

Butt in a sling

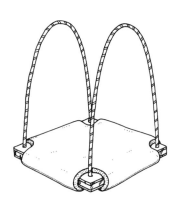

Butt in a sling. A comfortable and inexpensive belay seat.

Hanging belays are a pain in the butt, especially when you are the belayer. Save your ass by making a simple belay seat from a one-foot by one-and-a-half-foot rectangle of 1/2-inch plywood. Drill a hole in each corner and sling perlon through the holes to make a suspension system. For extra comfort, glue closed-cell foam to the "seat," making sure the foam extends slightly beyond the edge of the wood where your legs will bend over.

This "bosun's chair" is relatively light, easy to set up, and makes long belays far more comfortable.

— Onan J. Goat
Hell's Kitchen, New York

Hang 'em high

I needed a hanging stove, but my funds were low, so I decided to make one. I wound up spending $50: $40 for the stove (a Bleuet 206 cartridge model), and $10 total for a covered 3-quart saucepan, a 2-quart saucepan, 6 feet of small chain, a pack of S hooks, and a key ring. If you already have a cartridge stove you can retrofit that model for just $10.

To start, remove the handles from both saucepans. The 3-quart pot will be the wind-screen and hanging portion, so drill out a hole in the center of it just large enough for the stem of the burner. Unscrew the burner from the stove nozzle, stick the nozzle through the hole, and screw the burner back on.

Now comes the hard part: milling the slots in the bottom of the pan to accommodate the burner arms. Do that job by drilling a line of 3/8-inch holes for each burner arm, and then mill the holes together with a dremmel tool (a file will work). Once that's done, drill four larger air holes in the bottom.

Now drill three holes equidistant around the rim of the

saucepan, and crimp an S hook into each one. Cut the chain into three equal lengths and crimp the S hooks to the chain. Finally, feed the key ring through the ends of the three chains to serve as your clip-in point. Done right, the stove and pan should hang level, and the smaller two-quart saucepan should sit neatly inside.

— Mark Synnott
Jackson, New Hampshire

Improvised micro-cam

Aiding out thin expanding cracks is one of the most un-nerving and delicate aid-climbing maneuvers. While small camming devices work most of the time and are preferred over pitons there are still cracks too small to accept even the tiniest cam. In these instances a knifeblade or Lost Arrow stacked against a wired nut is an improvised version of a micro-cam, and is more secure than a piton alone, as this placement actually tightens as the crack expands.

To use this set-up, nest a wired nut against the back side of a piton near the tip, and then slip them together side-by-side in the crack (practice will tell you which size nuts and pins to use). Holding the placement steady, drive the piton up and simultaneously tug lightly downward on the nut which will cam against the piton blade (again, practice will tell how far to drive the pin). Clip the nut only, and test the piece carefully. Sometimes the nut will slide down and tighten as you weight it, so don't panic if it moves a little. Clip the eye of the pin with a keeper sling in case the placement blows, but whatever you do, don't load the pin. With practice this technique can become an invaluable tool for taking some of the terror out of these normally frightening placements.

— Duane Raleigh
Milton Falls, Colorado

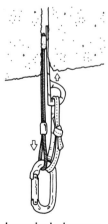

Improvised micro-cam.
Weight the nut only.

Shock therapy

When you're climbing with a partner, a hard lead fall often lifts your belayer a short distance. This dynamic action reduces the shock load on the leader's protection, increasing its chances of holding. A roped solo climber can achieve a similar effect by integrating the haulbag into the self-belay system.

Here's how you do it. Four or five feet above the main belay, clip the haulbag to a couple of equalized, bombproof pieces. Tie the end of the lead rope into the main belay anchors as you normally would. Pull two or three feet of slack between the belay knot and the haulbag, then clip the lead rope to the bag with a figure-8 knot. Now, clip the lead rope through the protection using your standard rope-soloing method. If

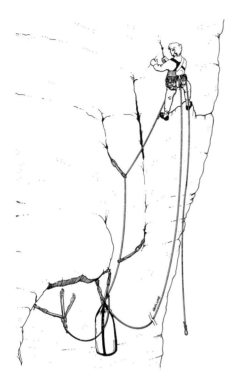

Shock therapy. Take the shock out of your solo belay by hanging the haulbag in front of your main belay anchors.

you fall, the haulbag will lift a few feet, just as your belayer would if he were there, before the load transfers to the belay anchor. The degree of load reduction depends on the haulbag's weight and the length of slack from the belay to the bag.

As with all roped-solo techniques, this one demands that you pay strict attention to detail. Too much slack between the bag and belay anchor will make it hard for you to jumar back up the rope after a fall, or worse, too much slack can let the haulbag lift so far it pulls out on the anchor.

— *Mike Adams*
Charlotte, North Carolina

Identity crisis

On a big wall, little mistakes, like grabbing the wrong size pitons off the rack, can add up, and cost you days if not the climb. Knowing what size pin fits where comes with experience, but even fried wall vets can get the baby angles confused with the 5/8-inch ones, and the #1 Lost Arrows mixed up with the #2s.

Eliminate that blunder by color-coding your pitons. For example, spray paint the baby angles bright red, the 5/8-inch angles electric blue, the 3/4-inch (standard) angles black, and so on until all your pins, from thin blades to the Lost Arrows, have a distinctive color that you can identify in a glance.

— William Holmes
Portland, Oregon

Knots and ropes

Glue you

Kevlar cord is nice for slinging SLCDs, Stoppers, and hexes, but because Kevlar is flame-resistant, whipping its ends is very difficult.

Super-type-glue provides a quick, long-lasting fix. Trim the ends of the cord with sharp scissors or a knife and roll the cord between fingers to work the kern flush with the mantle. Saturate the ends, inside and out, with several drops of glue. Let the glue dry overnight, and make sure it does not stick to anything.

— *Philip Reynolds*
Provo, Utah

The dirt on rope care

The dirt on rope care. Avoid bleach and detergents.

You are a filthy swine. But it's not all your fault. It's your rope. Every time you handle that thing it covers you with black soot. And if what the experts say is true, your grimy rope wears out much faster than a clean one ... so in a sense, you are paying for that bad Al Jolsen look.

How does your rope get so dirty? A couple of stories circulate. Manufacturer A says that the black on your rope is aluminum that rubbed off your carabiners. Manufacturer B says the rope's dry coating attracts dirt. It doesn't really matter who is right. The real issue is, what can you do about it?

Well, ropes aren't underwear. You can wash them. Here's how.

If you don't have a washing machine, uncoil your rope into a tub of cold water. Add soap. Do not use detergents, which will strip and dry out the nylon (detergents will always say "detergent" somewhere on the packaging). Woolite, Ivory Snow, and most natural shampoos are ideal.

Now hop in the tub and stomp around — pretend that you're crushing grapes for a hearty Bordeaux. Change the soapy water when it gets nasty and repeat until the water is clear. Rinse the rope thoroughly in clean, cold water.

If you have access to a washing machine, weave the rope into an "electrician's braid," which will keep the rope from snarling or being damaged by the agitator. Chuck the rope into the machine, add soap, and wash on the delicate cycle with cold water.

Keep in mind that detergents, bleach, and chlorine will damage your rope. If the washing machine's previous load of grimy duds were treated to any of these chemicals, run the machine through a cycle to rinse it. In the case of laundromats, assume that there's bleach in the machine and always run through a cycle to clean it out.

As a final step, you can recondition stiff, dry ropes by adding fabric softener to the rinse. Just don't overdo it or you'll end up with a flat, noodle rope.

To dry, leave the rope uncoiled in a warm, shady place. This can take several days, so plan ahead. When your rope is dry, use a ropebag to protect it from dirt and chemicals that can find their way into your backseat, trunk, or closet.

— *Bill Grigger*
Boulder, Colorado

Stacked

Have you ever stacked a rope in a sling only to have it tangle as you payed it out? Try stacking the rope so each successive bight is a bit shorter than the previous. This method prevents the bights from looping around each other and creating a mess.

Stacked. A snag-free rope stack.

— *Keith Pankow*
Santa Cruz, California

Hosed

When rigging fixed lines where you have unavoidable sharp edges, protect your ropes with homemade edge guards. Take 18-inch lengths of tough garden hose, slit these lengthwise, punch a hole in each end, and tie a keeper cord through the hole. Slip the hose over the rope any place it runs over an edge. Secure the hose in place by tying a prusik above it on the rope and clipping the keeper loop to this. When you jumar, simply jump your ascenders over the hose, just as you'd do a piece of gear or a knot. The first person on rappel removes the hose; the last person down puts it back on once she is just below the edge.

— *Mark T. Johnson*
Lander, Wyoming

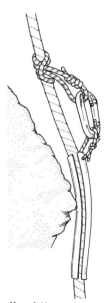

Hosed. Use garden hose to protect fixed ropes.

Tying one off

How you tie off that pin, bush, icicle, or chockstone often determines whether it will hold. While using tie-offs seems a simple enough task, a surprising number of climbers botch the job. They use the wrong knot or webbing, and as a result do little, if anything, to help the integrity of their pro. Here's how to do it right.

Forget bulky rope and cord. Flat, tubular webbing is the only suitable material for tie-offs. For aid climbing, strong and durable 11/16-inch "supertape" is popular among neophytes, but wall vets prefer the thin 1/2-inch webbing because it bites down on pins better. Half-inch webbing, however, cuts easily — it often gets trashed after only one use — and only holds around 1000 pounds. Double up 1/2-inch webbing on crucial pieces. For tieing off ice screws, supertape, because it is strongest, is the webbing of choice.

The three tie-off knots are the clove hitch, slip knot, and girth hitch. The clove hitch is the knot that's least likely to open up and slide off a pin, but then, because it's a wide knot, it doesn't place the load as close to the rock or ice as the trimmer slip knot. Use the clove hitch when tie-off security is

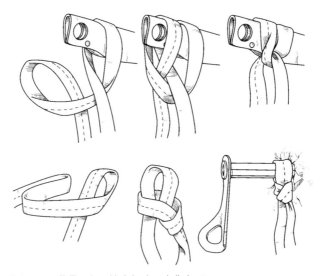

Tying one off. The clove hitch (top); and slip knot.

more of a worry than losing a few pounds of holding strength, which is most of the time.

The slip knot is notorious for loosening and falling off your pro (doubly so when there's an outward pull on it), but is the least levering of the knots. Use it on sketchy aid pieces where every pound counts (tip: angling your piton eyes up will help the slip knot stay put), and to tie off bolts or rivets that are too tight to the rock to take a girth hitch. Another excellent use of the slip knot is to pre-tie it over your ice screws. The pre-tied sling saves a step when you're on lead, minimizes leverage, and often saves you from having to chop a rotation path for the hanger.

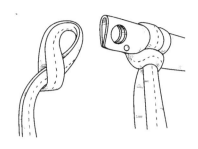

Tying one off. The girth hitch.

The girth hitch is a ratcheting knot that's ideal for clamping down on knobs and horns, and because it can be looped around objects, is ideal for tieing off chockstones, trees, and icicles. Further, because the girth hitch doubles over itself, it is the strongest of the three knots. The disadvantages of the girth hitch are that, like the clove hitch, it doesn't seat as close to the rock as you sometimes want, and it has a propensity to loosen when it isn't weighted.

— *David Littman*
Park City, Utah

All cut up

Cut any rope or webbing lately? Wish you had one of those nice hot cutters all the climbing shops have? Dream no more: cut webbing or rope using a hot soldering iron; get the kind with a wire-element tip, which sells for around $10. To make the cut easier, hammer the wire tip flat, so it has a sharper edge than the stock round one.

— *Stephen Van Leir*
Portsmouth, Virginia

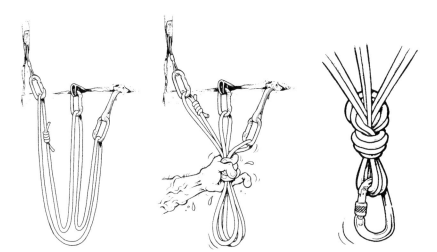

Untangling the web. Drape 'em, gather 'em, and tie 'em.

Illustration: Mike Clelland

Untangling the web

It is a common scenario. You arrive at a belay, fire in the anchors, then spend an eternity chaining quickdraws and slings together in an attempt to rig an equalized station.

After countless loosening of knots, adjusting sling lengths, and retightening knots, you still don't have it right. You have a mess. Worse, now that you've burned up a big loop of the lead rope, the leader is going to come up short on the next pitch. Frustrated and antsy, you give up and clip the tangle together, thinking, well, the anchor system isn't perfect, but it'll probably do.

Probably, but why risk it? With minimal fuss and forethought, and in less time that it takes you to applaud your splendid lead, you can construct an equalized anchor virtually every time you set up belay. We're talking cordelette.

The cordelette is a 20-foot length of 7mm perlon cord, tied runner style into a large open loop. To use, clip the loop to every point of protection you want in the belay, pull a leg down from each placement, and ponytail these so they all bottom out at the same low point. Last, tie all the loops together with a figure-8 knot, and clip yourself to the bottom loops. Done. Took you about 30 seconds.

Advantages of the cordelette are many. First, provided the load stays centered, it equalizes all the protection, and does so without the potential for a shock load if a piece fails, unlike other equalizing systems like the popular but dangerous "sliding X." Second, it is redundant at all points — even the loops you clip to are doubled; tripled if you have three pieces of gear. Finally, the cordelette is lightweight, packs small, doesn't eat up lead rope, and keeps things nice and tidy at the belay.

— Duane Raleigh
Milton Falls, Colorado

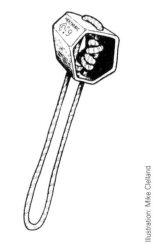

Hidden hex

Sometimes when placing a hex nut, the knot in the cord can be too big to fit in a thinner section of the crack below the piece, making a solid placement difficult.

On the larger size hexes — #8 and up — try tying the knot inside the nut. Leave about two inches of tail on each side of the knot and tuck these toward the inside of the hex.

— Mike Clelland
Driggs, Idaho

Hidden hex. A sneaky way to hide your hex knot.

Illustration: Mike Clelland

Pop tops

Here's a time-tested way to keep the knot on your haul line from abrading. Take a 12- or 16-ounce plastic soda bottle and cut the bottom off. Thread the rope through the neck, tie the rope to the haul bag, and slide the bottle top down over the knot, where it can act as a shield.

— Bob Roy Ramery
Brooktondale, New York

Improved prusik.

Improved prusik

In emergency rope-ascending situations where prusik knots are used in lieu of jumars, clipping a carabiner through the bottom loop of the knot and around the rope, and then passing the knot's upper tail through the carabiner prevents the knot from jamming, and allows it to slide easily once it has held weight. When possible use webbing (it's usually stronger and lasts longer) instead of perlon cord. Also, this version of the prusik knot is one-directional, as opposed to regular prusik knots, which work in any direction.

— *Vladimir Prochazka, Jr.*
Liberec, Czech Republic

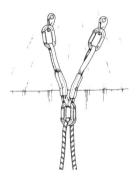

So tubular. Cheap-o sling protectors.

So tubular

Slide two short lengths of one-inch tubular webbing over slings to reduce wear when the sling runs over an edge in toproping situations.

— *Vance Atkins*
Tacoma, Washington

No slip cover

Tubular webbing rope protectors will slide down the rope — where they will no longer protect your rope. Prevent this scenario by crimping the middle of the rope protector. Fold over the edge of the webbing so it is snug on the rope, and glue it in place with Barge cement. I use a vice to hold the crimp while it dries.

— *Nicholas Jelen*
Glastonbury, Connecticut

Safety first

When I have to jumar a fixed line that's anchored at both ends, prohibiting me from tying a backup knot below the ascenders, I clip a carabiner through the top hole of my Petzl ascenders (you can't do this with some brands) to keep the rope from slipping out the crack between the cam and frame. As a further precaution, I tie a prusik knot on the rope just above each ascender and clip this to the carabiner. The prusiks slide easily as the ascenders push them up, and will lock should an ascender accidentally pop off the rope.

— *Jon Rubinfier*
Sherman Oaks, California

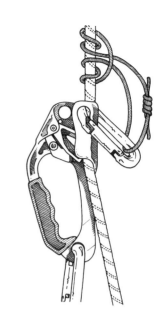

Safety first. The easy way to back up your ascenders.

Knot again

If you tie in and then fall or hang on the rope, getting the knot untied can be hard, as it's now cinched down super snug. Here's how to prevent this: when you tie in, thread the rope through your harness tie-in points twice as shown. That way, the extra loop of rope, not the knot, takes much of the load.

— *Mike Brown Jr.*
New York, New York

Knot again.

Rappelling

Out of a jam

Here's a trick for getting ropes to pull that are stuck due to friction at the anchor, or, in the case of a snow/ice bollard, melting and refreezing. Pull steadily and very hard — full bodyweight — on both ropes. Release the end of the rope that will pull through the anchor and continue to weight the side you want to pull down. The recoil of the unweighted rope should free it.

— *Mark T. Johnson*
Lander, Wyoming

Arresting one liners. Use a carabiner on your leg loops to generate more friction, or turn your figure 8 around and thread through the small hole.

Arresting one liners

After getting a head start on the next day's climbing, it's time to head back down to the bivy. You're a little nervous about rappelling that single 9mm, but the weight of the hanging rope is giving you lots of friction, so off you go. Halfway down, however, it's a different story: your hands are clenched in a death-grip, the hip of your pant leg is smoking, and the skinny rope is still slipping through your rappel device like a greased eel. By the time you reach the ledge, your palms are red, your knuckles are white, and you decide that next time, you'll fix a fat hawser.

Or, you could employ one of these nifty tricks for getting a grip on single-line rappels: if you use a figure 8, try rigging it upside down. Thread the rope through the smaller hole and clip your harness into the big one. Other climbers may look at you like you just stepped off the bus from Duluth, but you'll have the last laugh with the added control this tighter configuration provides.

For other rappel devices, you can feed the hanging rope through a carabiner clipped to your harness leg-loop. Raising the rope against this biner will generate additional braking power.

Finally, if your partner is already down, have her give you a "belay." All she must do is loosely hold onto the rappel line. If things get out of control during your descent, she can stop you simply by pulling down firmly on the rope.

— *David Pagel*
Duluth, Minnesota

Arresting one liners.

Rapping with different-diameter ropes

We all know that you can get the chop a dozen different ways rappelling. Anchor failure and rapping off the ends of your ropes are the obvious ones. A less obvious way was revealed to me late one night as I watched a friend bounce down the descent slabs, trailing both the rap lines behind.

My friend had the good luck to land on a ledge. He lived, and as we bandaged his mangled hands we pieced together what happened. We were rappelling on a pair of ropes of different diameters, an 11mm and a 7mm. A thinner rope, as it turns out, either because it stretches more or generates less friction in the rappel device, speeds through the device faster than a fatter rope. The result is that you arrive at the end of the thinner rope before the end of the fatter one. Not good. Making matters worse, if the connecting knot is on the side of the thicker rope, the knot travels down the wall, further shortening the thinner rope.

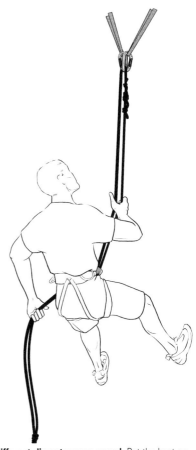

Different-diameter rope rappel. Put the knot on the thin rope's side of the anchor.

To prevent either scenario, tie the ends of the ropes together. As another backup, place the knot joining the two ropes on the same side of the rappel ring as the thinner rope. Do this, and the knot will jam against the anchor, preventing it from creeping down the wall. If circumstances prevent you from taking either precaution, gripping the thinner-diameter rope tighter that the fatter rope will help to even out the ends.

— *Sean Easton*
North Vancouver, Canada

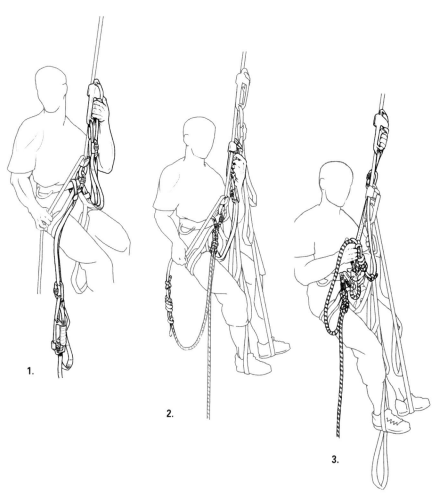

Downward bound. 1. Get your ascenders ready before you begin the rappel. 2. Just before you arrive at the knot, attach the lower ascender and weight it. 3. Remove the unweighted rappel device and place it below the knot.

Downward bound

Knowing how to rappel past a knot is one of the basic wall-climbing skills, yet is often a source of confusion, delay, and sometimes death. What follows is a well proven, safe, and efficient technique for dealing with those pesky knots.

Let's say you are on a wall and your fixed ropes are tied end to end and free hang without any intermediate anchor stations, a common situation. To rappel past the knot you will need a pair of ascenders (or prusiks), daisy chains (or runners), and aiders (or runners hitched together to form aiders).

Before you begin the rappel, arrange the ascenders, daisy chains, and aiders on the rope exactly as you would if you were going to jug a pitch, with one exception: leave the bottom ascender off the rope, and clip it to the side of your harness or let it hang out of the way. Place your rappel device on the rope below the top ascender, and rappel using the top ascender as a safety.

As you approach the knot, stop a couple feet above it. As a backup, pull up a bight of rope about six feet below the knot, tie an overhand figure 8, and clip yourself in. Now, with your free hand, snap the bottom ascender on the rope just above your rappel device. Once the device is free, remove it and put it on the rope below the knot. Down jug until your weight transfers back onto the rappel device, then remove the bottom ascender, jump the top one past the knot, and continue the rappel — don't forget to untie the backup knot well before you get to it.

— *Pete Takeda*
Boulder, Colorado

All rapped up

Have you been in a situation where you worried about an inexperienced or injured partner hooking in the rappel the wrong way? To ease your anxiety, clip two rappel devices on the rope at the same time. Use the bottom rap device for yourself, and clip your partner to the top one. Now you can rappel first, confident that your partner is clipped in correctly. Once you get to the next station or the ground, you can belay your partner by holding the rap ropes, and tugging on them when you need to slow his rappel.

— *Nick Hancock*
North Fork, California

All rapped up. Putting your partner's rappel device on the rope above you can prevent any snafus.

Twisted

Ever tried to escape a route in the rain, with cold hands, wishing your rappel device gave just a little more friction? Try putting a twist in the rope above the device, and then clip one end of a quickdraw (or runner) around the twist and the other end to a gear or belay loop on your harness. The crossed ropes and carabiner will give you more friction, and the carabiner will straighten out the ropes.

— *Lisa Morgan*
San Francisco, California

Twisted.

Double no trouble

You're rappelling a route, which because of the distance between anchors, requires two ropes. It's going smooth, but when you pull the ropes at one station a block comes down and partly chops one of the lines. What do you do?

Back up that untrustworthy rope by tying the two ropes together using figure-8 knots on a bight. Next, clip a carabiner through the knot loop on the good rope, and then clip the carabiner to the running portion of the same rope. Be certain to place the knot on the side of the anchor so that you always pull the bad rope to retrieve the rappel. Now if that bad rope fails, the carabiner and knot will cinch around the anchor and save you, although with only one rope left you'll likely be stranded.

— *Roger W. Laurilla*
Revelstoke, Canada

Double no trouble.

Pig rodeo

Rappelling with a pack or haulbag can be complicated and dangerous. A common mistake is to try and wear the pack on you back. A light pack doesn't present a problem, but staying upright with a heavy pack is a struggle, and can fatigue you to the point where you lose control of the rappel.

There is a simple solution: Clip a long runner to the pack or bag, and then clip the runner to the belay/rappel loop on your harness, and rappel as normal. This keeps the bag out of the way by your feet, and lets the rappel device, not you, take the load.

— *Orval Sowder*
Eugene, Oregon

Pig rodeo. Let your rappel device bear the load.

Smooth move

If you use a Black Diamond ATC or Lowe Tuber for rappelling, you have probably noticed the large amount of friction these devices generate makes the rappel jerky and difficult. There is a simple solution: attach an extra carabiner to your harness and clip it to the rappel rope in conjunction with the one you normally use with the rappel device. The additional carabiner widens the radius the rope runs over, giving you a smoother rappel.

— *Jim Capra*
Tacoma, Washington

Ice, mixed, and mountaineering

Bale necessity

Duct tape, Barge cement, and baling wire are staples in anyone's expedition repair kit — with these three items, you can fix almost anything, from a broken stove to a ripped tent fly.

Besides its usefulness for all-around repairs, baling wire makes an economical and effective instep strap for your gaiters. Cut a 12-inch piece of wire, twist an end around one of the grommets in your gaiter, then adjust the length for a snug fit and attach the other end. Trim any excess wire, and for the truly finished look, wrap the twisted attachment points with duct tape.

Baling wire is stiffer that nylon cord or neoprene straps, so stepping into the gaiters is usually a breeze. It's strong and wears well, even when you're walking on scree. It doesn't freeze or ball up with snow and ice. And when you need to replace it, baling wire is cheap and readily available.

— Michael Kennedy
Carbondale, Colorado

Get a grip. Convert your fingerboard for winter training.

Get a grip

Several years ago I realized that I needed to get stronger if I wanted to hang on and put in gear on steep ice routes. First, I tried simulating the pulling-down motion of ice tools by draping towels over a chin-up bar. Later, I switched to wood dowels, which feel more like ice-tool shafts. To do the same, drill holes through the dowels an inch or so from one end.

Thread a loop of cord through the holes and wrap the handles with tape. Fasten the "tools" to a chin-up bar or fingerboard, then lock off and imagine good gear.

— *Kevin Cooney*
Boulder, Colorado

Short tooling

Most technical ice tools are 50 centimeters or so long. This yields about 40 centimeters of reach, but robs you of the same amount of reach when you do a low "lock off." For most ice climbs, the disparity is inconsequential, but on steep mixed terrain the difference can spell failure.

Even the score by choking up on the tool shaft. Though not a completely new development, choking up, or "short tooling," has found a new application on radical mixed climbs where the cruxes are often reachy.

Short tooling involves sliding your hand up the tool shaft. The better the pick placement the easier you'll find this maneuver. On dicey dry-tool placements you can use both hands on one tool to walk hand-over-hand up the shaft. Beware of choking up too high — you'll lever out on the shaft and pop the placement. Practice this and other dry-tool maneuvers on you local choss pile or after hours in the gym, if the manager allows such strangeness.

— *Pete Takeda*
Boulder, Colorado

Digging in

A secure tent is important on big mountain routes. Tying the guy lines down helps the tent to flap less in the wind, giving you a better night's sleep. At windy and exposed campsites, digging tents in is important as there have been instances where a tent, complete with occupants, has blown off the mountain. You can either place your tent in a dug-out enclosure or surround it with a wall of snow blocks at least as tall as the tent. Small stuff sacks filled with snow and buried like Deadmen provide strong tie-off points for guy lines. Ski poles, ice axes, helmets, and ice screws can all be used as Deadmen; pull on the anchor to make certain it's solid.

— *Conrad Anker*
San Leandro, California

Be prepared

Beyond the hazards of the fall itself, crevasse self-rescue can be frustrating and exhausting. You can simplify one of the first steps in the process — removing and tying off your pack — by adding a 5-mm perlon "ripcord" to your pack. To do this, tie a loop of perlon around your pack's shoulder straps so that you have a 4-foot loop. Tuck the loop under the top lid. Now when you fall in a crevasse you have an easy-to-reach loop that makes tying off your pack less of a hassle.

— *Mike Daniel*
Rochester, New York

Be prepared. Make a 5-mm perlon loop "ripcord" for your pack.

Bright idea

Budget expedition? Make cheap, high-visibility wands by folding 2-inch-wide reflective tape (from 3-M, etc.) over garden bamboo wands available in lawn-garden centers. These wands cost almost nothing and show up in the beam of you headlamp.

— *David Ehlers*
Dayton, Ohio

Cheers

At the crags trying to impress that styling babe with a sophisticated Sauvignon, but you forgot the corkscrew? Lucky for you, you do have a #2 RP (a small Stopper also works). Push the cork in. Yes in. Stick the nut in the bottle and drag the cork out. Ba-ba-bing!

— *Nigel Robinson*
Ottawa, Canada

Cheers. A makeshift cork popper.

Light your fire

Tired of getting caught without matches for the stove? Fix that by adding a Coleman sparker, available for around $3 most anywhere that sells Coleman stoves. Experiment with the sparker to determine where it needs to be positioned to work best with your stove, then bolt it securely. You may have to drill a couple of holes, but having a stove that's sure to fire up, even when it is wet, is worth the effort.

Light your fire.

— *Anthony Maler*
North Ogden, Utah

Flatland technology

Your ice tools are dull, so you dig out your old ski file. Trying to steady your ice axe with one hand, you awkwardly begin filing the blunted tip you smacked against the rock while climbing verglas. But with another tool and a pair of crampons to go, you're not relishing the time-consuming job ahead. There's a better way to go.

With a basic clamp-on "prairie" hand grinder, available at hardware stores, you can hone your tools to a razor's edge in seconds. Don't grind too zealously, though, as overheating the metal can weaken it. When you hit the road to Ouray or Banff, be sure to throw your grinder in the trunk.

— *Michael Benge*
Carbondale, Colorado

Polar solar

Use solar power to make your drinking water when you're out in the cold. Do this by covering your plastic water bottle with black tape to absorb sunlight. Cram the bottle with clean snow, and then fill it to the brim with water to get the melting process underway. Strap the bottle to the outside of your pack and refill with snow as necessary. On a sunny day this technique can make three quarts of water with minimal effort and saves your precious stove fuel.

— Gene Pires
Bellingham, Washington

Look what's shaking

Here's a trick that works better than a heat exchanger or holding a lighter to a stove cartridge to make it work in cold weather. Take a shake-and-heat handwarmer and hold it to the bottom of the cartridge with a piece of elastic cord. To hold in the heat, slip a small round of Ensolite around the cartridge base and under the elastic. Be sure to cut air holes because the heater needs oxygen to work.

— Mike Dimitri
New Paltz, New York

How's this grab ya?

When making a V-thread anchor to rappel off ice, most people use a stiff wire to snag and retrieve the threaded cord. To eliminate this tedious task, go to your local hardware store and buy a "grappler," a one- or two-foot-long, spring-loaded rod with a retractable claw. This device makes grabbing and keeping the cord a cinch.

— Gene Pires
Bellingham, Washington

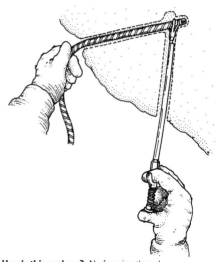

How's this grab ya?. No-fuss ice thread.

Ice breaker

Removing ice protection can be harder than placing it, especially in extremely cold temperatures. This is because ice pitons and screws melt the ice slightly when they are placed; as the meltwater refreezes it locks the protection in place.

To break this bond, hit the head end of the protection once or twice as if you were trying to drive the piece deeper. The force of the blows will break the ice, making removal easier.

— *Thomas W. Kopp*
Onalaska, Wisconsin

Jump start

You are on a long winter route and remembered your trusty Petzl Kangaroo Pouch to keep your headlamp battery warm, but your partner didn't. Take a shake-and-heat and cram it (tightly) on the side and top of his battery. The battery cover may not close completely, but the heater will keep it working in the cold.

— *Steve Truitt*
Golden, Colorado

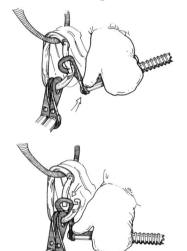

Racked with envy

Getting ice screws off your rack when you're wearing gloves or mittens is tough. To make the job easier, rack your screws on extra large, bent-gate carabiners with the gates facing down and out. Thus racked, you can remove screws with a gloved hand by merely pressing the hanger against the gate.

— *Paul Cording*
Hillman, Minnesota

Racked with envy.

Can you dig it?

Here's a way to convert a Deadman snow fluke and ice axe into a workable shovel.

Get one U-bolt that will just slip over the shaft of your axe, and a regular bolt that will fit through the hole at the bottom of your axe shaft. If your axe doesn't have a bottom hole, get two U-bolts. Get wing nuts for every bolt.

Center the Deadman on the axe shaft and mark the places where the bolts will hit it. Drill out those spots, push the bolts through, tighten down the wing nuts, and you're ready to dig.

— *Asby Parva*
Leicestershire, England

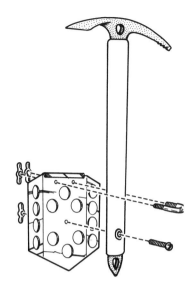

Dig it. U-bolts and wing nuts convert an ice axe and a snow fluke into a shovel.

Screw off

When an ice screw doesn't go in all the way, you need to tie it off. But messing with a tie-off while on lead is a hassle. Simplify this before getting on the ice by taking a sewn quickdraw and threading the screw through one of the carabiner loops. This way the tie-off is already in place, and you can clip the screw as soon as it is partly in — boosting your waning confidence.

A word of caution: make sure the quickdraw fits snugly around the screw shaft, and also check to insure that the quickdraw can't slip over the screw's eye.

— *Joe Redshirt*
Yosemite, California

Screw off. Pre-thread your ice screws with quickdraws for hassle-free tie-offs.

Keener image

On long alpine and mixed routes, you can keep your tools sharp with a six-inch steel file snapped in half, or a fish-hook file (cost about $2.50), available at sporting-goods stores.

— Conrad Anker
San Leandro, California

Get the point

We all know about keeping our ice-tool picks sharp, but did you know that a few minor pick modifications can greatly increase your tools' performance on mixed terrain?

The first step is to file down the point of the pick to reduce its profile. A lower profile point will slip into those tiny pockets, creases, and bottlenecks. Next, file the underside of the tip into an aggressive hook that will guarantee a precision bite on the smallest edge.

As with all modifications, experiment, and stay within the limits of comfort. You can always whittle more away, but you can never put it back.

— Pete Takeda
Boulder, Colorado

Taping leashes

The game of modern mixed climbing is often played on vertical to overhanging rock decorated with intermittent ice smears. Such terrain quickly generates a grotesque forearm pump. Minimize the pain by taping your tool leashes to the shafts.

To tape your leashes, choose a point just past halfway down the tool shank. Wind a few wraps of duct tape around the tool body and leash. Done right, the leash will still give you enough mobility to manipulate gear, make clips, and easily retrieve the tool back into your hand. Taping half way down the shank also lets you "choke up," a key maneuver when you short tool.

— Pete Takeda
Boulder, Colorado

Save your axe

Rappelling down snowfields presents problems, the biggest of which is anchors. You either have to leave behind expensive pickets or flukes, or, if snow conditions allow, cut bollards. There is a better way — use your ice axes and rig them so they can pull down with the ropes.

Here's how you do it. Trench one tool horizontally, like a Deadman, several inches in the snow. Next, tie a five- to 10-foot length of 6- or 7-mm perlon through the hole in or near the spike of the second tool, and drive that tool vertically into the snow so it is behind and supported by the horizontal axe. Now thread the perlon through the hole in the head of the horizontal tool. Tie your ropes together and thread them around the vertical axe. If you are rappelling with one rope, thread it likewise, but tie an overhand knot on one side just below the axe head. Finally, take a 6- or 7-mm prusik and hitch this on the rope below the knot and attach it to the perlon on the axes.

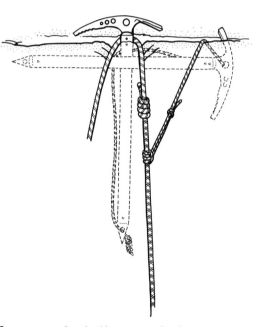

Save your axe. A retrievable snow rappel anchor.

Rappel, then pull the strand that has the prusik on it. The prusik will jam against the knot, lifting out the vertical axe, which in turn pulls out the horizontal axe. Make sure you are wearing a helmet, and watch your head as the axes come tumbling down.

As with all snow anchors, make sure the snow is firm enough to support an anchor and practice plenty in a low, safe area before you set up a rappel for real.

— *Bela G. Vadasz*
Norden, California

Double your vestibule on snow

On multi-day snow climbs there is never enough room in the tent — especially for double boots, crampons, and packs. Double the "cold storage" of your tent by digging a hole in the area beneath the vestibule. The hole will increase storage space and keep your gear protected during stormy weather. Plus, you can now sit upright in the door and dangle your legs into the hole, a handy position for cooking and putting on your crampons without sticking it to your tent.

— *Penn Newhard*
Basalt, Colorado

Anti-freeze water

Climbing in the winter poses a serious problem: your water supply freezes. The obvious solution is to wrap your water bottles with old closed-cell foam and duct tape (be sure you make a foam lid), but less known is the trick of burying your water bottles a foot or so in the snow, which will act as an insulator. Sounds preposterous, but I've used this technique for 30-below nights in Alaska and Maine, and it works.

— *John Gartner*
Hollis, New Hampshire